Post-quant Cryptography

Defending Against Quantum Threats

Taylor Royce

DEDICATION

To everyone dedicated to the advancement of cybersecurity and protecting the integrity of our digital world, this book is dedicated. A safe and secure future is built on the commitment of the researchers, engineers, and visionaries who put in endless effort to protect our systems from new dangers.

Additionally, it is devoted to individuals who welcome the task of comprehending intricate issues and their capacity to influence our digital environment. May the future generation of cybersecurity experts be motivated to take on the issue of protecting against quantum threats by using this book as a resource and guide for anyone navigating the ever evolving field of cryptography.

Lastly, this book is dedicated to the future of digital security, for which we all work to create a more secure and safe future.

DISCLAIMER

This book's content is solely intended for informational and educational purposes. Although every attempt has been taken to guarantee the content's accuracy and dependability, the author and publisher make no guarantees or assurances about the content's completeness, accuracy, or applicability.

The knowledge in this book may become out of date as new developments in the rapidly developing fields of post-quantum cryptography and quantum computing take place. When making judgments about cybersecurity and cryptography, the reader should seek professional assistance and examine additional sources.

Any repercussions resulting from the use or reliance on the information included in this book are not the responsibility of the author or publisher. Before adopting or offering advice on cryptographic systems or security measures, readers should use their own discretion and prudence.

The thoughts and viewpoints presented in this book are

those of the author and may not represent those of any institution, business, or organization with whom the author may have affiliations.

CONTENTS

ACKNOWLEDGMENTS

I want to express my sincere gratitude to everyone who helped to make this book possible. Above all, thanks to the outstanding scholars, cryptographers, and cybersecurity professionals whose pioneering work in post-quantum cryptography established the groundwork for this subject. Your commitment and inventiveness are still motivating and influencing the direction of digital security.

I would especially like to express my gratitude to my friends, mentors, and coworkers who offered priceless advice, criticism, and encouragement during the writing process. Your support, knowledge, and helpful criticism have been crucial in honing the material and bringing this book to life.

Additionally, I would like to thank the many organizations, such as the National Institute of Standards and Technology (NIST), and the international research groups that are putting forth endless effort to create and standardize quantum-resistant cryptography methods. The security of our digital world depends on your contributions.

I want to express my gratitude to my family and friends for their patience and belief in my work, as their continuous support and understanding allowed me to concentrate on this project. Your support has consistently served as a source of inspiration.

Finally, I want to sincerely thank all of the people who have read this book. It is my goal that the information presented here will enable you to participate in the group effort to protect against quantum attacks and successfully traverse the quickly changing field of cybersecurity.

CHAPTER 1

POST-QUANTUM CRYPTOGRAPHY OVERVIEW

1.1 Recognizing Quantum Computing's Danger

A Synopsis of Quantum Computing and Its Capabilities

In terms of computer technology, quantum computing is a paradigm change. Quantum computers use qubits, which take advantage of the concepts of superposition and entanglement, as opposed to classical computers, which process data in binary bits (0s and 1s). This makes it possible for quantum computers to execute intricate computations at rates that are not possible for classical systems. For example, a sufficiently powerful quantum computer may factorize a big number in a matter of seconds, but a classical computer might take years to do so.

The Dangers of Quantum Computers to Traditional Cryptography

The computational difficulty of tasks like factoring huge

2

integers or computing discrete logarithms is the foundation of the majority of modern cryptography systems, including RSA and ECC (Elliptic Curve Cryptography). Because solving these problems would take an impractical length of time for traditional computers, they are considered safe. But quantum computers can address these issues considerably quicker by using algorithms like Shor's algorithm, making many traditional cryptography techniques outdated.

- For instance, 2048-bit RSA keys are now safe from traditional attacks, but quantum computers might easily crack them.
- Even if symmetric cryptography systems like AES are less susceptible, they nevertheless need far bigger key sizes to remain secure in the age of quantum computing.

The Need for Post-quantum Cryptography Solutions Is Critical

There is an urgent need for cryptographic systems that are immune to quantum assaults due to the predicted arrival of large-scale quantum computers in the coming decades. To guarantee that safe communications, financial transactions, and data storage systems are not jeopardized when quantum computers become a reality, the shift to post-quantum cryptography (PQC) must start immediately. Global projects like the post-quantum cryptography standardization project from the National Institute of Standards and Technology (NIST) have been sparked by this urgency.

1.2 Cryptography's Development

A Synopsis of Traditional Cryptography Techniques
Over millennia, cryptography has undergone tremendous change:

- **Ancient Times:** Simple character transposition or substitution was a feature of early encryption, like the Caesar cipher.
- **20th Century:** The mechanical cryptography era was best represented by the Enigma machine.
- **Modern Era:** Symmetric methods such as DES (Data Encryption Standard) and later AES (Advanced Encryption Standard) were made possible by the advent of computer-based

encryption.

Symmetric to Asymmetric Cryptography Transition

In the 1970s, asymmetric cryptography emerged as a solution to the drawbacks of symmetric cryptography, especially the requirement for secure key exchange. Public-key systems, such as RSA, revolutionized industries like digital signatures, e-commerce, and secure online banking by enabling safe communication without the need for prior key sharing.

The Reasons Why Traditional Cryptography Is at Risk in the Quantum Era

The foundation of traditional cryptography techniques is the computational impossibility of particular mathematical issues. This presumption is profoundly challenged by quantum computing:

- While Grover's technique is less destructive, it can accelerate brute-force assaults on symmetric systems, thereby halving the security strength of key sizes. Shor's algorithm successfully factors huge numbers and computes discrete logarithms, compromising RSA and ECC.

Therefore, a new cryptography basis that is independent of existing mathematically precarious structures is required in the quantum age.

1.3 Post-quantum Cryptography Definition

Details on Post-quantum Cryptography

Cryptographic techniques created to resist attacks from both classical and quantum computers are referred to as post-quantum cryptography (PQC). PQC modifies current cryptographic frameworks to withstand quantum computing risks, in contrast to quantum cryptography, which uses the ideas of quantum physics to provide secure communication.

- Reliance on mathematical issues that are thought to be challenging for quantum computers, such as lattice-based problems and hash-based constructs, is one of its key features.
- It can be used practically on current digital infrastructures without the need for quantum technologies.

The three main goals are compatibility, scalability, and security.

PQC algorithms seek to meet a number of important needs:

1. **Security:** Keeping robustness against classical risks while guaranteeing resilience against quantum attacks.

2. **Scalability:** Algorithms must continue to perform well even when key sizes or computational complexity are raised.

3. **Compatibility:** Smooth interaction with current communication protocols, guaranteeing a seamless transfer without requiring significant system overhauls.

The Function of Complexity in Mathematics in Post-quantum Algorithms

PQC makes use of computationally demanding mathematical constructions for both classical and quantum systems. Several well-known contenders are:

- **Lattice-based cryptography:** Makes use of issues such as the Shortest Vector Problem (SVP), which even quantum algorithms are unable to solve.

- Built on error-correcting codes, code-based

cryptography provides resilience against quantum attacks.

- The complexity of solving multivariate quadratic equations is the foundation of multivariate polynomial cryptography.

While each of these strategies has different trade-offs in terms of practical deployment, key size, and performance, taken as a whole, they show how secure communication will develop in the quantum age.

We can gain a greater knowledge of the difficulties and advancements propelling the field of post-quantum cryptography by comprehending these fundamental concepts. The following chapters will examine particular algorithms, practical uses, and international initiatives influencing the shift to a cryptography environment that is quantum-resilient.

CHAPTER 2

CRYPTOGRAPHIC VULNERABILITIES AND QUANTUM COMPUTING

2.1 The Operation of Quantum Computing

Superposition and Quantum Bits (Qubits)

The qubit, the quantum equivalent of the classical bit, is at the core of quantum computing. A qubit can exist in a superposition of both states at the same time, in contrast to a conventional bit, which can only exist as either 0 or 1. This implies exponential parallelism, where a quantum system with n qubits can represent 2^n states simultaneously.

Qubits also take advantage of entanglement, a quantum phenomena in which two qubits' states are inextricably linked, independent of distance. Because fewer operations must be processed sequentially, computation can proceed more quickly.

For example:

- When assessing a 10-bit system, a classical computer may evaluate one of 1024 states simultaneously.
- The ability of a quantum computer to analyze all 1024 states at once significantly increases processing efficiency.

The Implications of Quantum Algorithms for Data Processing

Specialized algorithms that tackle complicated problems tenfold quicker than their classical counterparts are made possible by the particular mechanics of quantum computing. Important algorithms consist of:

- **Shor's Algorithm:** Threatens the basis of RSA and ECC encryption by effectively factoring big integers and computing discrete logarithms.
- **Grover's Algorithm**: Reduces brute-force attack times by a square root factor, speeding up unstructured search issues.

By altering computing paradigms, these algorithms make it

possible to make advances in fields like encryption, materials science, and optimization. Their consequences for safe communication, however, emphasize how urgently cryptographic innovation is needed.

Several organizations are spearheading the development of quantum computers, as evidenced by the following examples:

- **IBM's Quantum System One:** A commercially available quantum computer intended for study and testing.
- **Google's Sycamore Processor:** Prove "quantum supremacy" by resolving a problem in a matter of seconds that would have taken thousands of years for traditional supercomputers.

Instead of universal quantum computing, D-Wave Systems concentrated on quantum annealing for optimization challenges.

Although large-scale quantum computers that can crack cryptographic systems are not yet commonplace, these developments highlight the fact that their continual development is a warning flag.

2.2 The RSA Vulnerability and Shor's Algorithm

Outlining the Features of Shor's Algorithm

Peter Shor created Shor's algorithm in 1994. It is a quantum method that solves discrete logarithms and factors integers quickly, two operations that are computationally impossible for conventional computers to perform for large inputs. Its strength is in using modular arithmetic's periodicity to calculate factors exponentially more quickly than with conventional techniques.

- For instance, it would take billions of years to calculate a 2048-bit RSA modulus using traditional techniques. This may be completed in hours or even minutes if Shor's algorithm were run on a strong enough quantum computer.

The Reasons RSA Encryption Is in Danger

The difficulty of factoring big numbers is the foundation of RSA's security. However, once quantum computers reach a certain scale, RSA encryption may become outdated due to the exponential speedup provided by Shor's method.

- With keys of 2048 or 4096 bits, current RSA encryption offers strong defense against traditional brute-force assaults.
- These key sizes would be inadequate for an error-corrected quantum computer with thousands of logical qubits.

Proposed Timetable for Quantum Computer-Based RSA Decryption

Although projections differ, experts anticipate the following:

- Within the next five to ten years, small-scale quantum computers that can crack simple RSA keys (like 512-bit ones) may become available.
- Within 15 to 30 years, large-scale, fault-tolerant quantum computers that pose a threat to 2048-bit RSA could be created, contingent on improvements in scalability and error correction.

This possible timetable emphasizes how urgent it is for businesses to switch to post-quantum cryptography techniques.

2.3 Symmetric Cryptography and Grover's Algorithm

The Effect of Groover's Algorithm on Brute-Force Attacks

In contrast to Shor's method, Grover's approach speeds up unstructured search activities rather than focusing on particular mathematical issues. When N is the size of the keyspace, it lowers the time complexity of brute-force assaults on cryptographic keys from $(O(N))$ to $O(\sqrt{N})$.

For instance:

- 2^{128} operations are needed to perform a traditional brute-force attack on a 128-bit symmetric key.
- Grover's technique makes previously secure keys more vulnerable by reducing this to roughly 2^{64} operations.

The Possible Need for Longer Keys in Symmetric Cryptography

Longer key sizes are required in symmetric cryptography

in order to defeat Grover's algorithm. To preserve comparable security standards in a quantum computing environment, the National Institute of Standards and Technology (NIST) advises:

- Expanding AES key length from 128 bits to at least 256 bits.
- To maintain robustness, symmetric algorithms that are no longer in use are being replaced.

Using Updated Symmetric Protocols to Reduce Risks

To counteract quantum concerns, the cryptographic community is constantly creating and improving symmetric protocols:

- For instance, switching from AES-128 to AES-256 offers a strong defense against Grover's square root speedup.
- Layered defenses can be produced by combining post-quantum algorithms with symmetric encryption in hybrid cryptographic systems.
- **Regular Important Updates:** The window of vulnerability to brute-force attacks, whether quantum or otherwise, is decreased by routinely rotating keys.

In addition to being a scientific wonder, quantum computing poses a significant challenge to cryptography. The demand for quantum-resilient solutions is greater than ever since Grover's method threatens symmetric cryptography and Shor's technique jeopardizes RSA and ECC. The basis for creating and implementing post-quantum cryptography standards, which guarantee secure communication in the quantum era, is an understanding of these flaws and their consequences.

CHAPTER 3

POST-QUANTUM CRYPTOGRAPHY FUNDAMENTALS

As quantum computing advances, post-quantum cryptography stands at the forefront of secure communication. The mathematical ideas, quantum-safe algorithms, and hybrid approaches that support the shift to quantum-resilient cryptographic systems are explored in depth in this chapter.

3.1 Foundations of Mathematics

Post-quantum cryptography's strength is its dependence on mathematical problems that are impervious to both quantum and conventional attacks. Its development is centered on the following domains:

- **Lattice-Based Cryptography:** This technique takes advantage of the intricacy of issues like the Learning With Errors (LWE) and Shortest Vector Problem

(SVP) challenges. These issues form the basis of post-quantum solutions since they are thought to be immune to quantum attacks.

Important features of lattice-based cryptography include:

- **Efficient Algorithms:** Compared to certain classical systems, lattice-based schemes frequently allow for speedier encryption and decryption procedures.
- Digital signatures (like Dilithium) and key exchange protocols (like Kyber) are examples of versatile applications.
- Strong resistance to quantum algorithms is ensured by the reductions to worst-case hardness of many lattice-based algorithms.

Cryptography Based on Code

The challenge of decoding general linear codes, which is still computationally impossible even for quantum computers, is the foundation of code-based cryptography's security.

- Examples of notable encryption systems include the **McEliece Cryptosystem:**, which has been thwarting attacks since its inception in 1978.

- **Excellent Key Exchange Performance**: Provides quantum robustness for session key exchange, but at the expense of increased storage needs.

Benefits include a decades-long track record of security. For some specific use situations, such as secure communication with embedded devices, it is feasible.

The Cryptography of Multivariate Polynomials

The challenge of solving systems of multivariate polynomial equations over finite fields is the foundation of multivariate cryptography.

Features consist of:

- **Digital Signatures:** Programs like Rainbow are effective for verification and signing procedures.
- Compact keys are frequently used in multivariate systems, which makes them appropriate for resource-constrained applications.
- These systems exhibit resilience against known assaults, including those involving classical and quantum computation.

Challenges: Certain schemes are susceptible to structural and algebraic attacks, which calls for cautious use and ongoing evaluation.

3.2 Safe Algorithms for Quantum

Thorough attempts are being made to find and standardize algorithms that are immune to quantum attacks in order to counter the vulnerabilities presented by quantum computing.

An Overview of the Algorithms Suggested by NIST

The Post-Quantum Cryptography Standardization Project was started by the National Institute of Standards and Technology (NIST) in order to assess and suggest quantum-safe algorithms. The following applicants have been identified as the top solutions following several evaluation rounds:

- **Public-Key Encryption and Key Exchange:** Kyber (based on lattices) provides robust quantum resistance and great efficiency.
- **Digital Signatures:** Falcon and Dilithium, both

lattice-based, provide strong security and functionality.

The significance of rigorous testing and standardization is paramount.

- For post-quantum algorithms to be widely used and to be secure and interoperable, standardization is essential. To find weaknesses, a thorough peer review is part of the process.
- Testing in the real world to assess performance in various scenarios.
- Cooperation between government agencies, business, and academia to develop useful applications.

The following criteria are used to evaluate algorithms for quantum resistance:

1. **Security:** Resistance to both classical and quantum attacks.
2. **Efficiency:** Speed and resource consumption for signature, encryption, and decryption processes.
3. The capacity to manage different degrees of computing demands is known as scalability.

4. **Implementation Complexity:** Integration into current systems is simple.

NIST highlights the need for adaptability and advises businesses to use algorithms that may change with the cryptographic environment.

3.3 Cryptographic Hybrid Solutions

It will take time to make the switch to post-quantum cryptography. A viable way forward is provided by hybrid cryptography systems, which combine post-quantum and conventional techniques.

Combining Post-quantum and Classical Methods

In hybrid techniques, post-quantum algorithms (like Kyber and Dilithium) and classical algorithms (like RSA and ECC) are used concurrently. This guarantees that the other method offers a backup layer of protection even in the event that one is compromised.

- Quantum-safe features are introduced while maintaining compatibility with existing systems.
- For instance, dual-encryption techniques encrypt

data using both Kyber and RSA.

- ECC and Dilithium are combined in hybrid digital signatures to ensure validity.

Transition Strategies for Organizations To reduce interruptions, post-quantum cryptography adoption calls for a staged approach:

1. **Evaluation:** To find vulnerabilities, make a list of all the cryptographic assets that are currently in use.
2. **Preparation:** Create a plan for incorporating post-quantum solutions, giving high-risk systems priority.
3. **Implementation:** Start with hybrid solutions and work your way up to traditional approaches.
4. **Testing:** Keep an eye on system performance and make sure that it works with the rest of the system.

Assuring Future-Proofing and Backward Compatibility

For a smooth transition, backward compatibility is essential. Some strategies are:

- Maintaining support for classical algorithms throughout the migration process is a feature of dual-key systems.

- The development of cryptographic protocols that may be modified in response to new standards is known as "flexible protocol design."
- Assuring that new systems can coexist with legacy infrastructure without sacrificing security is known as interoperability testing.

Proactive steps are necessary for future-proofing:

- Consistently tracking quantum computing developments to foresee threats.
- Keeping up with NIST and other standardizing bodies' revisions.
- To keep up with changing threats and solutions, cryptographic agility is an investment worth making.

Making the transition to post-quantum cryptography is a challenging but essential task to protect digital communication in the quantum age. Organizations can successfully manage this shift by comprehending the mathematical underpinnings, deploying hybrid cryptography solutions, and embracing NIST-recommended algorithms. Adopting these preemptive measures will guarantee resilience against new attacks and safeguard sensitive data integrity for many years to come.

CHAPTER 4

Post-quantum Cryptography Standardization Initiatives

The shift to post-quantum cryptography (PQC) is a complex process that calls for strong standardization efforts in addition to being a technological undertaking. This chapter discusses the difficulties in attaining the widespread adoption of quantum-safe standards, emphasizes international cooperation, and examines the crucial role played by organizations that set standards, such as the National Institute of Standards and Technology (NIST).

4.1 NIST's Function in Cryptographic Standards

For many years, NIST has led the way in cryptography standards, offering rules that support safe communication networks all across the world. One important step in future-proofing digital infrastructure is its ongoing effort to standardize post-quantum cryptography.

The Post-quantum Cryptography Project at NIST: An Overview

NIST's Post-Quantum Cryptography Standardization Project was started in 2016 with the goal of identifying and formalizing cryptographic methods that are resistant to quantum computer assaults.

The initiative's objectives are to:

- Create algorithms that are impervious to both classical and quantum attacks.
- Verify that the chosen algorithms are effective and cross-platform implementable.
- Establish a clear path for businesses making the switch to post-quantum cryptography.

Selection Phases:

- 69 candidate algorithms were found after the first call for submissions.
- The pool was narrowed down to a few candidates after several review rounds that concentrated on digital signatures, key exchange, and public-key encryption.

Selection Criteria for Quantum-Safe Algorithms NIST assesses algorithms based on strict standards to guarantee their viability and robustness:

- **Security:** Defense against classical and quantum attacks, including extreme situations.
- Performance: Implementation is feasible on a variety of hardware, including IoT devices and high-performance servers.
- **Scalability:** The ability to adjust to various operating needs, notably those of large-scale applications.
- **Implementation Complexity**: Integration into current software libraries and systems is simple.

The state of standardization efforts as of right now

NIST has declared as of today:

- **Finalists and Alternates:** While some algorithms are undergoing further examination, others, such as Dilithium (signatures) and Kyber (encryption), are ready for standardization.
- **Next Actions:** In order to promote broad adoption, final standards and implementation guides are anticipated to be released in the upcoming years.

4.2 Global Cooperation

Global concerns about cryptographic security call for concerted efforts from governments, academic institutions, and business executives.

International Cryptographic Research Communities' Contributions

Researchers in cryptography around the world have been instrumental in the creation of post-quantum algorithms: University-industry collaborations have sped up the identification and examination of quantum-resistant methods.

- Open contests have promoted innovation by enabling researchers from many geographical areas to test and enhance candidate algorithms.

The Role of Organizations Like ISO and IETF In order to guarantee worldwide uniformity, standardization organizations other than NIST are essential:

- The International Organization for Standardization,

or ISO, is dedicated to developing globally recognized cryptographic standards that will enable safe international trade and communication.

- The Internet Engineering Task Force, or IETF, is responsible for incorporating post-quantum methods into popular internet protocols like Transport Layer Security (TLS).

- The European Telecommunications Standards Institute, or ETSI, investigates the use of quantum-safe cryptography in future quantum key distribution (QKD) systems and telecommunication networks.

Worldwide Security Effort Coordination To achieve worldwide quantum resistance, the following is necessary:

- **Unified Standards:** Preventing fragmentation by coordinating efforts across standards bodies.

- **Cross-Border Testing:** Making sure algorithms work well in a variety of technological and regulatory contexts.

- **Open Communication Channels**: exchanging information about implementation difficulties, vulnerabilities, and innovations.

4.3 Standardization Challenges

The process of standardization is inherently complicated, particularly when the underlying technology deals with changing threats.

Computer Efficiency and Security in Balance

Because quantum-safe algorithms frequently require more processing power, their mainstream adoption is hampered:

- **Performance Trade-offs:** On limited devices, such smartphones and Internet of Things sensors, algorithms must balance acceptable performance with quantum resistance.
- **Optimization Strategies:** Algorithms are still being optimized by research to lower latency and memory consumption without sacrificing security.

Ensuring Interoperability Across Systems To prevent incompatibilities, post-quantum cryptography must be smoothly integrated into current cryptographic systems:

- **Legacy Systems:** Since many modern systems

depend on well-established protocols like RSA and ECC, it is difficult to completely replace them.

- **Hybrid Solutions:** Introducing hybrid systems that provide backward compatibility during the transition phase by combining classical and quantum-safe approaches.

- **Standardized libraries and APIs:** Creating universal software interfaces and libraries can make industry adoption easier.

Resolving Opposition to Implementing New Standards

There are several causes of adoption resistance, such as:

- **Cost Issues:** Upgrading or replacing cryptographic infrastructure can be costly, particularly for smaller businesses.

- Adoption may be postponed by some stakeholders in anticipation of additional validation or advancements in post-quantum algorithms.

- **Awareness Gaps:** Businesses that are not aware of the dangers that quantum computing poses could not give updating their cryptography systems first priority.

Techniques for overcoming opposition include:

- **Education and Awareness:** Organizing outreach initiatives to notify interested parties of the pressing need to switch to quantum-safe technology.

- Governments and business leaders might provide grants, tax exemptions, or certifications to companies who implement quantum-safe technology as a way to encourage early adoption.

- **Gradual Migration Plans**: Offering precise plans and resources to enable small-scale improvements with the least amount of disturbance.

Standardizing post-quantum cryptography is a monumental task requiring global collaboration, rigorous evaluation, and proactive strategies to overcome challenges. NIST's leadership, coupled with international partnerships, is paving the way for a secure cryptographic future. By addressing technical, logistical, and cultural hurdles, the cryptographic community can ensure that digital infrastructure remains resilient against emerging quantum threats.

CHAPTER 5

POST-QUANTUM CRYPTOGRAPHY IMPLEMENTATION IN ENTERPRISES

Organizations need to be proactive in moving their systems toward post-quantum cryptography (PQC) solutions as the emergence of quantum computing approaches. A thorough road map for identifying vulnerabilities, organizing migration plans, and creating a strong quantum-safe environment is given in this chapter. To guarantee that digital infrastructures are secure without needlessly disrupting operations, PQC deployment calls for careful design, testing, and execution.

5.1 Evaluating Current Cryptographic Frameworks

Assessing the organization's present cryptographic systems is the first step in putting post-quantum cryptography into practice. An efficient transition strategy is built upon this assessment, which offers a clear awareness of weaknesses.

Finding Infrastructure and Protocol Vulnerabilities

Popular cryptographic techniques that support the security of modern digital systems, such RSA, Diffie-Hellman, and ECC (Elliptic Curve Cryptography), are under risk from quantum computers. Companies need to pinpoint the locations where these algorithms are used:

- **Encryption:** Examine the protocols used to secure internet connections, such as TLS/SSL.
- Analysis of systems that use digital signatures to confirm identities is part of the authentication process.
- **Key Exchange:** Determine how encryption keys are safely shared across systems.

Businesses can map out their risk exposure by evaluating cryptographic reliance on weak algorithms.

Giving Communication Channels and Sensitive Data Priority

Not every communication and data channel is equally

important. Systems security should be prioritized by organizations according to the following criteria:

- **Sensitivity:** Determine high-value assets, such as financial data, trade secrets, and customer information.

- Systems that communicate with external networks should be evaluated since they are more vulnerable to security breaches.

- **Longevity:** Pay attention to protecting information that needs to be kept secret for a long time, including medical records or court paperwork.

Making a Cryptographic Dependency Inventory

A methodical approach to mitigation is made possible by a comprehensive inventory of cryptographic dependencies. Important actions consist of:

- Keep track of all the encryption and authentication techniques that are being used.

- **Identifying Integrations:** Take note of any dependencies on external hardware, software, or libraries for cryptographic functions.

- **Recording Use Cases:** Recognize how business

processes and workflows incorporate cryptography solutions.

This inventory will serve as a starting point for creating and putting into practice quantum-safe solutions.

5.2 Strategies for Migration

Making the switch to post-quantum cryptography calls for a calculated strategy that strikes a compromise between resource limitations, operational continuity, and security.

Incremental vs. Complete Migration Methods

Depending on the goals and capabilities of the company, one of two primary migration approaches may be used:

- The gradual substitution of quantum-safe algorithms for susceptible ones is known as "incremental migration."
- It reduces implementation risks by enabling ongoing testing and modification.
- Ideal for big businesses with intricate systems and little tolerance for downtime.

Complete Migration:

- A comprehensive redesign of cryptographic systems in a single, well-coordinated endeavor.
- Faster implementation, but if not carefully planned, there is a greater chance of operational disruption.
- Smaller organizations or systems with few interdependencies are the best candidates.

Difficulties with Cryptographic Library Updates

There are some difficulties in making the switch to quantum-safe cryptography:

- **Compatibility Issues:** Outdated software or hardware constraints may make it difficult for legacy systems to incorporate new methods.
- **Increased Resource Requirements:** A lot of post-quantum algorithms require more processing power, which could mean that infrastructure needs to be upgraded.
- **Staff Training:** To properly comprehend and apply post-quantum cryptography techniques, IT teams may need extra training.

In order to overcome these obstacles while preserving functionality and security, organizations must set aside resources.

The Value of Implementation in Phases

Implementing changes gradually lowers the risks involved in significant changes. Important actions in a phased approach consist of:

1. Quantum-safe algorithms should be implemented in controlled conditions to assess their compatibility and performance.

2. **Critical Systems First:** During the early stages, give top priority to protecting sensitive data and high-value systems.

3. **Feedback Loops:** Gather input continuously and adjust tactics in light of results.

4. **Gradual Rollout:** In later stages, extend deployment to less important systems.

Organizations can handle unforeseen problems without endangering overall security by implementing changes in stages.

5.3 Establishing an Ecosystem That Is Quantum Safe

Post-quantum cryptography implementation calls for the development of an entire ecosystem that promotes long-term security and adaptation, not just the replacement of algorithms.

Post-quantum Cryptography Integration with Applications

- To guarantee smooth operations, post-quantum cryptography needs to be smoothly included into organizational workflows and applications.
- The ability of quantum-safe algorithms to communicate with current application programming interfaces (APIs) is known as "API compatibility."
- **Multi-Platform Support:** Adapt solutions to a variety of contexts, such as mobile platforms, cloud services, and Internet of Things devices.
- Work together with hardware and software providers to integrate quantum-safe standards into their goods and services.

System robustness is increased and disturbances are reduced with proper integration.

Ensuring Adherence to Changing Rules

It is probable that regulatory frameworks will change to require quantum-safe cryptography standards. Companies need to:

- **Remain Current:** Keep an eye on updates from regulatory agencies like NIST, ISO, and GDPR.
- **Conduct Audits:** Examine systems on a regular basis for adherence to quantum-safe standards.
- To prove compliance with regulatory standards, keep thorough records of all cryptographic changes.

Organizations can avoid fines and maintain their competitiveness in their industries by practicing proactive compliance.

Constant Watching and Updates

- For post-quantum cryptography to continue to be

effective against new threats, it needs constant maintenance.

- **Security Assessments:** Regularly check how resilient quantum-safe algorithms are to emerging flaws.
- Keep up with developments in post-quantum cryptography research and incorporate better algorithms when they become available.
- **Incident Response:** Create procedures for promptly resolving security lapses or flaws in quantum-safe settings.

Long-term protection is ensured and a proactive security culture is fostered by ongoing monitoring.

Post-quantum cryptography implementation is a complex process that calls for careful preparation, calculated execution, and constant attention to detail. Establishing a thorough quantum-safe environment that promotes compliance and adaptation, implementing phased migration plans to guarantee seamless transitions, and evaluating present systems to find weaknesses are all necessary for organizations. Businesses can protect their digital infrastructures from quantum threats while preserving consumer trust and operational continuity by implementing these measures. In the quantum era, the consequence of inaction could be disastrous, therefore now is the moment to take action.

CHAPTER 6

CRYPTOGRAPHY BASED ON LATTICES

A key component of post-quantum cryptography is lattice-based cryptography, which provides strong defense against quantum attacks. This chapter examines the mathematical underpinnings of lattices, looks at well-known algorithms in this framework, and assesses the benefits and difficulties of putting lattice-based cryptography systems into practice.

6.1 Overview of Lattices

Using intricate mathematical structures that are impervious to attacks by both classical and quantum computers, lattices are essential to the development of quantum-resistant encryption methods.

The Definition of Lattices and Their Function in Cryptography

The integer linear combinations of a collection of basis vectors in a multidimensional space form a regular grid-like structure called a lattice. A lattice Λ in R^n can be defined mathematically as follows:

$\Lambda=\{a1b1+a2b2+\ldots+anbn \mid ai \in Z\}$

Where b1,b2,…,bn are the basis vectors.

Lattices are used in cryptography because of their intrinsic complexity. Even with quantum computers, it can be quite challenging to solve some computational tasks inside these structures. Lattice-based cryptographic systems are based on this complexity, which guarantees their protection from upcoming quantum attacks.

The Quantum-Resistant Nature of Lattice-Based Cryptography

Quantum algorithms like Shor's can effectively tackle issues like integer factorization, which are a prerequisite for classical cryptographic methods like RSA. However, lattice-based cryptography relies on mathematical problems whose structure prevents them from being solved by quantum computers.

Important features include:

- **High Dimensionality:** Lattice issues get progressively more complex with dimension, making quantum methods useless.

- The absence of an effective quantum algorithm Polynomial-time solutions to problems such as Learning with Errors (LWE) and the Shortest Vector Problem (SVP) are not available on quantum computers.

Lattice-based cryptography is a favored option for post-quantum cryptography systems because of these characteristics.

Principal Mathematical Issues Employed

1. Leaning with mistakes (LWE):

- It entails resolving a set of linear equations that are noisy.

- Because it is difficult to retrieve the original equations from the noise, it is secure.
- serves as the foundation for key exchange protocols and encryption techniques.

2. Shortest Vector Problem (SVP):

- Finding the shortest nonzero vector in a lattice given its basis is the task of the Shortest Vector Problem (SVP): The cryptographic security of the problem is based on its exponential complexity in high dimensions.

These issues guarantee that lattice-based cryptography provides strong security and adaptability.

6.2 Common Algorithms Based on Lattices

Within the lattice-based framework, a variety of algorithms have been created that provide solutions for key exchange, digital signatures, and encryption.

NTRUEncrypt and Applications

One of the first lattice-based cryptosystems for encryption and decryption is NTRUEncrypt.

Design Principles:

- Generates cryptographic keys by combining modular arithmetic and polynomial rings.
- Because of its simplicity, it can be implemented effectively on devices with limited resources.
- Use in secure communications, particularly in embedded systems and Internet of Things devices.
- It provides a balance between computing efficiency and security.

Kyber: An Algorithm Suggested by NIST

- In the NIST post-quantum cryptography standardization process for key encapsulation mechanisms (KEM), Kyber has become a prominent contender.
- The Learning with Errors (LWE) problem serves as the basis for the following salient features.
- Strong security guarantees and useful efficiency are provided.

Benchmarks for Performance:

- Achieves low latency and great throughput in key exchange protocols.
- Both high-performance systems and low-resource situations can benefit from it.

Real-World Uses and Performance Standards

- **Cloud Security:** Guarding against quantum risks to data exchanges in cloud contexts.
- Enabling post-quantum-secure communication protocols, such as TLS, is necessary for secure messaging.
- **Blockchain:** Strengthening blockchain systems' resistance to upcoming cryptographic flaws.

Performance benchmarks demonstrate competitive encryption speeds and modest resource consumption, highlighting the scalability of lattice-based cryptography.

6.3 Benefits and Drawbacks

Although it has drawbacks, lattice-based cryptography provides a strong defense against quantum flaws.

Lattice-Based Cryptography's Security Benefits

1. The first is Quantum Resistance:

- Protected from assaults by both quantum and classical computers.
- Based on issues for which there are no effective quantum algorithms.

2. Versatility:

- Supports a large number of cryptographic operations, such as homomorphic encryption, encryption, and signatures.
- Advanced features like safe multiparty computation are made possible.

3. Efficient Implementation:

- Kyber and other algorithms provide useful performance measurements appropriate for real-world applications.
- Designed for low-resource settings, such Internet of Things devices.

4. Robust Theoretical Underpinnings:

- Security is thoroughly examined and supported by decades of lattice theory research.

Implementation and Computation Cost Challenges

1. Key and Ciphertext Sizes:

- Lattice-based methods usually use more bandwidth than classical algorithms because they demand larger keys and ciphertexts.

2. The Computational Overhead:

- Higher processing costs for encryption and decryption.
- For optimum performance, hardware upgrades might be required.

3. Complexity in Integration:

- It may require a lot of resources to modify current systems to accommodate lattice-based methods.
- For correct implementation and upkeep, certain knowledge is needed.

Possible Improvement Areas

1. Algorithm Optimization:

- Cutting down on the amount of the ciphertext and keys without sacrificing security.
- Through hardware acceleration, computing efficiency can be increased.

2. Standardization Efforts:

- NIST and other organizations are always researching ways to simplify lattice-based cryptography standards.

3. User-Friendly Implementations:

- Creating tools and libraries that make it easier to integrate with current systems.

A strong and adaptable foundation of post-quantum security is lattice-based cryptography. It provides a dependable defense against quantum threats while enabling sophisticated cryptographic functions by taking advantage of the intrinsic complexity of lattice problems. Its usefulness is being improved by continuous research and optimization efforts, despite obstacles like bigger key sizes and processing overhead. Lattice-based cryptography will be essential to protecting digital infrastructures as quantum computing develops, guaranteeing long-term resilience and trust in a world enabled by quantum technology.

CHAPTER 7

CRYPTOGRAPHY BASED ON CODE

A key component of post-quantum cryptography is code-based cryptography, which uses error-correcting codes' characteristics to protect data from both quantum and classical attacks. This field, which has a history that dates back to the late 1970s, has shown itself to be a promising choice for quantum-resistant algorithms since it provides both practicality and robustness. The historical background, important algorithms, and potential and challenges of implementing code-based cryptography are all covered in this chapter.

7.1 Foundations and History

Error-correcting codes, a commonly used idea in communication systems to rectify transmission faults, and cryptography cross to form the foundation of code-based cryptography.

The McEliece Cryptosystem: The History of Code-Based Cryptography

- The earliest use of code-based cryptography was the McEliece cryptosystem, which Robert McEliece unveiled in 1978.
- The system employs a public key that is produced from a generator matrix of a particular error-correcting code, usually a Goppa code.
- The original generator matrix and decoding data are contained in the private key.
- Random errors are added to the message during encryption, and the private key is used to repair problems during decryption.
- The security of the cryptosystem is based on the difficulty of decoding a random linear code, which is an NP-hard task.

Despite the fact that quantum computing was still theoretical at the time, McEliece's design was groundbreaking in its resistance to quantum attacks.

Error-Correcting Codes' Function in Cryptography

Code-based cryptography systems are based on error-correcting codes, such as LDPC (low-density parity-check) codes, Reed-Solomon codes, and Goppa codes.

Error Correction Principles:

- Redundancy is used in data encoding to identify and fix transmission faults.
- Over noisy channels, the procedure guarantees dependable communication.

Related to Cryptography:

- Code-based cryptography renders unauthorized decryption computationally impossible by purposefully creating faults during encryption.

Important Properties of Quantum Resistance

Code-based cryptography is quantum-resistant due to its inherent characteristics:

- **Difficulty of the Decoding Problem:** For big, random linear codes, quantum methods, such as

Shor's and Grover's, do not significantly improve decoding performance.

- **Large Key Size:** Although this presents a problem, even with quantum computers, brute-force assaults are not feasible due to the large key size.

Its robustness is further supported by the fact that decades of research have not discovered effective ways to attack well-designed code-based systems.

7.2 Algorithms Based on Post-quantum Codes

Modern code-based cryptography has developed into a set of algorithms tailored for post-quantum applications, building on McEliece's pioneering work.

NIST-Reviewed Algorithms

For assessment, the NIST Post-quantum Cryptography Standardization Project has selected a number of code-based algorithms:

1. A modernized version of the original McEliece cryptosystem is known as Classic McEliece:

- Binary Goppa codes, which provide a good mix

between security and efficiency, are used.

- **Strengths:** Excellent encryption and decryption performance and a track record of security.
- Large key sizes, usually hundreds of kilobytes, are a weakness.

2. BIKE (Bit Flipping Key Encapsulation):

- Based on quasi-cyclic codes, enabling reduced key sizes compared to Classic McEliece.
- Its effective decoding methods make it appropriate for contexts with limited resources.

3. Hamming Quasi-Cyclic, or HQC:

- It makes use of quasi-cyclic codes and seeks to strike a compromise between computing efficiency, key size, and security.
- The main encapsulation techniques for safe communications were the focus.

The scalability, real-world applicability, and quantum resistance of these algorithms are rigorously tested.

Secure Communications Applications

Code-based cryptography works especially well for applications that need to be extremely resilient and secure:

- **Military and Government Communications:** Preventing future quantum threats to secret information.
- **Satellite Communication Systems:** Using cryptography and error correction to protect long-distance communications.
- **IoT Devices:** Ensuring safe communication in contexts with limitations.

Actual Deployment Situations

- **Email Encryption**: Secure email protocols like S/MIME can incorporate code-based cryptosystems.
- **Secure File Storage:** Protecting private information kept on cloud servers or in distributed systems.
- **Public Key Infrastructure (PKI):** Substituting quantum-safe algorithms for classical ones that are susceptible, such as RSA.

Code-based algorithms are excellent choices for crucial

applications in the quantum age due to their adaptability and demonstrated security.

7.3 Adoption and Difficulties

Notwithstanding its potential, code-based cryptography has real-world issues that need to be resolved before it can be widely used.

Challenges in Implementation

1. Key sizes that are large:

- Compared to classical systems, code-based cryptosystems McEliece in particular require noticeably bigger keys.
- Logistical challenges arise in the storage and transfer of keys, particularly for devices with limited resources.

2. Performance Considerations:

- Although encryption and decryption procedures are effective, high-throughput applications may require improvement.

3. Algorithm Complexity:

- Developing and executing code-based algorithms calls for specific knowledge of error-correcting codes as well as cryptography.

Bandwidth and Storage Considerations

1. Increased Resource Requirements:

- Large public keys require more bandwidth for transmission and use more memory.
- In resource-constrained contexts, like IoT networks, this could be an issue.

2. Impact on System Design:

- In order to support code-based cryptography, existing systems might require major architectural adjustments.

How Companies Are Getting Past Obstacles

Organizations and scholars are using a number of tactics to solve these issues:

Optimized Key Representations:

- Public keys are compressed without sacrificing security.

- Reducing size by utilizing structured and quasi-cyclic coding.

Utilizing specialized hardware, like FPGAs or GPUs, to speed up encryption and decryption procedures is known as "hardware acceleration."

Phased Integration:

- To reduce disturbance, gradually switch from classical algorithms to code-based systems.

Standardization Efforts:

- NIST, ISO, and industry stakeholders have worked together to create precise adoption guidelines.

A seasoned and dependable method of post-quantum security, code-based cryptography is built on decades of study and real-world application. Its acceptance is being facilitated by continuous improvements in algorithm design, hardware optimization, and standardization, even though obstacles like big key sizes and computational complexity still exist.

Code-based cryptography provides a tried-and-true and scalable way to secure vital systems and communications as quantum computing develops. It will continue to be an essential part of the cryptographic landscape in a world enabled by quantum technology because of its special combination of error correction and cryptographic strength.

CHAPTER 8

MULTIVARIATE POLYNOMIAL CRYPTOGRAPHY

A promising area of post-quantum cryptography is multivariate polynomial cryptography, which takes use of the computational difficulty of resolving systems of multivariate polynomial equations over finite fields. This chapter analyzes the fundamental ideas of this method, looks at important multivariate polynomial-based algorithms, and assesses the difficulties and opportunities for development in this field.

8.1 Fundamental Ideas

The foundation of multivariate polynomial cryptography (MPC) is the intrinsic difficulty of resolving nonlinear polynomial equation systems. MPC uses algebraic structures that are computationally difficult for both classical and quantum computers to crack, in contrast to many traditional cryptographic techniques that rely on number-theoretic difficulties.

Overview of Problems with Multivariate Polynomials

The challenge of solving a system of multivariate quadratic equations over a finite field is at the core of MPC.

The Problem's Structure:

In the following formula, a multivariate polynomial is written as follows:

- $P(x_1, x_2, \ldots, x_n) = \sum_{i,j} a_{ij} x_i x_j + \sum_i b_i x_i + c$, where a_{ij}, b_i and c are coefficients within a finite field. A set of such equations must be satisfied by $x_1, x_2, \ldots, x_n$.

Computational Challenge:

- This problem is known to be NP-hard and is frequently referred to as the Multivariate Quadratic problem (MQ). Even using quantum techniques like Grover's search, it is impossible to solve efficiently due to its exponentially increasing complexity with the number of variables.

Why Quantum Computers Struggle to Solve These Issues

Problems having particular structures, such those that can be exploited by Shor's or Grover's algorithms, are well suited for quantum computers. The MQ problem, however, does not fit under any of these groups:

- The nonlinear character of polynomial equations is a challenge for quantum algorithms.
- **Exponential Growth:** As the number of variables and equations increases exponentially, so does the number of possible solutions, rendering brute-force approaches impracticable.
- Complexity is increased by the fact that operations are limited to finite fields.

Function in Encryption and Signature Systems

1. MPC works especially well in:

- Multivariate polynomials are used by schemes such as Rainbow and GeMSS to generate digital signatures in a secure and effective manner.
- Among its advantages are quick verification and signature, which makes them appropriate for real-time applications.

2. Encryption Systems:

- Because of its quantum resistance, MPC is used in some encryption methods, but less frequently.

These uses demonstrate how MPC can take the place of weak traditional algorithms in crucial security systems.

8.2 Multivariate Polynomials in Post-quantum Algorithms

Numerous multivariate polynomial-based cryptographic algorithms are being developed; some of these algorithms are potential candidates for the NIST post-quantum cryptography standardization process.

GeMSS and Additional NIST Prospects

GeMSS (Great Multivariate Short Signature) is a well-known example:

Design Philosophy:

- GeMSS combines strong security with low storage needs, making it ideal for brief digital signatures.
- It expands on a popular method in MPC called the Hidden Field Equations (HFE) framework.

Key Features:

- **Efficiency**: Moderate computing expenses and quick verification of signatures.
- **Security:** The MQ problem's complexity provides defense against both classical and quantum attacks.
- **Applications:** Fits well with blockchain systems, Internet of Things devices, and other settings that need low-power cryptography.

Some noteworthy multivariate algorithms are as follows:

1. Rainbow:

- A multi-layered polynomial equation signature system that improves security.
- High efficiency and flexibility to different security levels are among the advantages.

2. HFEv- (Hidden Field Equations with Variations):

- Additional randomization approaches are used to extend the HFE strategy in order to thwart particular attacks.

Secure Digital Signature Use Cases

Digital signatures benefit greatly from multivariate

polynomial cryptography because:

- **Compact Signatures**: Effective transmission and storage, particularly in resource-constrained contexts.

- **Quick Operations:** Minimal computing cost for verification and signature.

- In a post-quantum world, quantum resistance provides long-term security.

Among the uses are:

- **Authentication in IoT Devices:** Ensuring safe communication in gadgets with constrained processing capacity.

- **Secure Blockchain Transactions:** Preserving user identities and transaction integrity.

Evaluating Security and Efficiency

Efficiency and security trade-offs are crucial when assessing multivariate algorithms:

- **Efficiency:** Verification is usually faster than traditional techniques like RSA, despite the computationally demanding nature of signature generation.

- Appropriate parameter selection guarantees resistance to attacks, including those that employ quantum-specific techniques.

8.3 Difficulties and Prospects

Multivariate polynomial cryptography has a lot of obstacles to overcome before it can be widely used, despite its potential.

Scalability Restrictions

1. Key Size:

- Large public keys are frequently needed for multivariate systems, which raises the cost of transmission and storage.
- For gadgets with limited resources, like Internet of Things sensors, this could be an issue.

2. Computation Costs:

- The signature process can need a lot of resources, even while verification is effective.
- It is still quite difficult to strike a balance between

security and performance.

Integration with Current Frameworks for Cryptography

1. Compatibility Issues:

- The replacement of traditional algorithms such as RSA and ECC necessitates a significant overhaul of the current infrastructure.
- Adoption depends on ensuring a smooth connection with existing systems.

Hybrid Approaches:

- Multivariate cryptography can be used in conjunction with other quantum-safe techniques, including lattice-based systems, to improve overall security and adaptability.

Multivariate Techniques Research Advancements

The goal of ongoing research is to overcome the constraints and discover new possibilities:

1. Enhanced Key Management:

- Creating small key representations to save

bandwidth and storage requirements.

2. Enhanced Security Models:

- Improving the choice of parameters to increase defenses against changing attack methods.

3. Developing more effective signature generating methods to lower computing overhead is known as "optimized algorithms."

4. Standardization Efforts:

- NIST and other organizations' joint efforts to create strong multivariate cryptography standards.

A potent weapon in the post-quantum cryptography toolbox, multivariate polynomial cryptography provides a special fusion of security, efficiency, and quantum resistance. For digital signatures and encryption systems, it offers reliable solutions by taking advantage of the difficulty of solving nonlinear polynomial equations.

Even if issues like integration and scalability still exist, continuous improvements in algorithm design and execution are opening the door for wider usage. Multivariate polynomial cryptography will be essential to protecting digital ecosystems for many years to come as the quantum danger becomes closer.

CHAPTER 9

Post-quantum Cryptography's Practical Uses

Traditional cryptographic systems face serious difficulties as a result of the development of quantum computing, which calls for a switch to post-quantum cryptography (PQC). This chapter explores the practical uses of PQC in important industries, emphasizing how it can revolutionize the security of financial transactions, the protection of medical data, and the defense of the Internet of Things (IoT) against quantum attacks.

9.1 Protecting Monetary Exchanges

Because of its reliance on secure communications, encryption, and authentication methods, the financial industry is one of the most susceptible to cryptographic threats. For this important business to be future-proof, post-quantum cryptography is essential.

Dangers to Financial and Banking Systems

The cryptography techniques utilized in the following could be compromised by quantum computers:

1. Digital Banking:

- Online banking transactions are secured by public-key encryption. Current algorithms that are vulnerable to quantum assaults include RSA and ECC.

2. Payment Systems:

- To safeguard card information and customer data during transactions, payment gateways rely on secure cryptographic methods.

3. Financial Data Storage:

- Even though encrypted financial records are safe, they may be decrypted if they were stolen today and later targeted by quantum computers.

Widespread financial fraud, theft, and a decline in confidence in the global financial system could result from a successful strike.

Using Blockchain Post-quantum Techniques

Another area where quantum robustness is crucial is in blockchain technology, which is the foundation of cryptocurrencies and decentralized finance:

Present Dangers:

- Blockchains rely on digital signatures to secure wallets and validate transactions.
- Entire blockchain ecosystems could be compromised by the forging of signatures by a sufficiently powerful quantum computer.

Quantum-Safe Blockchain Protocols:

- PQC integration with blockchain protocols is being researched. For instance, safe substitutes for developing quantum-resistant digital signatures are provided by algorithms such as lattice-based cryptography.
- In order to maintain security throughout the transition period, some blockchain initiatives are experimenting with hybrid models that combine classical and post-quantum cryptography.

Making Sure Payment Systems Are Secure

Additionally, PQC can strengthen conventional payment systems by:

- **Integrating Quantum-Resistant Algorithms:** Replacing weak encryption techniques in online payment gateways and payment card networks.
- Strengthening identity verification through the use of quantum-safe digital signatures is one way to improve authentication mechanisms.
- Using lightweight PQC algorithms to provide secure transactions on devices with limited resources is one way to protect mobile payment systems.

To protect against upcoming quantum threats while preserving operational effectiveness and regulatory compliance, financial institutions must proactively implement PQC.

9.2 Medical Care and Information Security

The healthcare sector is a prime target for cyberattacks because it produces and stores enormous volumes of sensitive data. In a future afforded by quantum technology, post-quantum cryptography is essential to guaranteeing the security and integrity of healthcare systems.

The Value of Protecting Medical Records

1. Nature of Healthcare Data:

- Patient records, which include diagnoses, treatment plans, and medical histories, are extremely sensitive.
- Unauthorized access may result in patient safety risks, insurance fraud, or identity theft.

2. Quantum Risks to Healthcare Systems:

- Electronic health records (EHRs) that use conventional encryption techniques like AES and RSA are susceptible to quantum assaults.
- Patient information could be revealed retroactively if data collected now is later encrypted.

3. Post-quantum Solutions:

- By putting PQC into practice, patient records are protected even as quantum technologies advance.
- Large datasets can be effectively encrypted using algorithms like Kyber and FrodoKEM.

Medical Device Encryption Using Quantum Security

The Internet of Medical Things (IoMT), which is connecting medical equipment more and more, calls for strong security measures:

- Pacemakers and other implanted devices are examples of connected gadgets.
- Diagnostic tools like CT and MRI scanners.
- Tools for remote monitoring, such as fitness trackers and glucose sensors.

Dangers:

- Quantum assaults have the potential to compromise private patient information or interfere with device operation.
- The use of lightweight PQC algorithms guarantees secure communication between devices and central systems without using processing resources excessively.

Legal Obligations Regarding Data Privacy

- Strict laws like the HIPAA (Health Insurance

Portability and Accountability Act): require that patient health information be protected in the United States.

- **GDPR (General Data Protection Regulation)**: enforces strict data privacy laws in the European Union.

Organizations benefit from quantum-safe cryptography measures:

- **Achieve Compliance**: Make sure that changing data protection regulations are followed.
- **Prevent Penalties:** Steer clear of fines and harm to your reputation that can come from violations.

Healthcare providers can safeguard vital systems and increase confidence in their capacity to preserve patient privacy in a post-quantum world by incorporating PQC.

9.3 Post-quantum Cryptography and IoT

From household appliances to industrial gear, billions of objects are connected by the Internet of Things (IoT). Adapting to quantum-safe security presents special problems for this hyperconnected world.

Difficulties in Preventing Quantum Threats on IoT Devices

1. Limited Computational Resources:

- A lot of Internet of Things devices, such wearables and smart sensors, have little memory and computing power.
- It is quite difficult to implement sophisticated encryption algorithms on these devices.

2. Massive Attack Surface:

- The sheer volume of IoT devices makes it more likely that vulnerabilities will be taken advantage of.

3. Long Device Lifecycle:

- Since Internet of Things devices are frequently in use for years or decades, it is crucial that their cryptographic protocols be future-proof.

Simple Cryptography for Devices with Limitations

It is necessary to modify post-quantum cryptography to meet the particular requirements of IoT systems:

Lightweight PQC has the following features:

- Decreased computational complexity to accommodate constrained hardware capabilities.
- Optimized energy use for gadgets that run on batteries.
- Algorithms such as SPHINCS+ and Falcon are being investigated due to their lightweight and quantum-resistant characteristics.

Increasing IoT Ecosystem Resilience

To guarantee IoT networks' quantum robustness, the following is necessary:

1. Using post-quantum cryptography techniques to secure communication between devices and cloud systems is known as "end-to-end encryption."
2. Enabling remote updates to cryptographic methods guarantees that devices stay safe even when new threats appear.
3. **Hybrid Security Models:**
    - By combining post-quantum and classical techniques, a gradual shift can be made without jeopardizing ongoing operations.

4. Collaborative Efforts:

- To create standardized frameworks for quantum-safe IoT security, manufacturers, researchers, and governments must collaborate.

By tackling the issues raised by quantum computing, post-quantum cryptography has the potential to completely transform security in a number of vital industries.

PQC guarantees the integrity of payment networks, blockchain systems, and transactions in the finance industry.

- **In Healthcare**: It guarantees regulatory compliance, safeguards medical equipment, and preserves patient records.
- In the Internet of Things, lightweight cryptography solutions protect linked devices and increase ecosystem resilience.

Adopting post-quantum cryptography is becoming essential as quantum technology advances, not only a safety measure. Organizations may strengthen their systems against new risks and preserve operational excellence and trust in the digital age by proactively integrating PQC into these domains.

CHAPTER 10

CRYPTOGRAPHY'S PROSPECTS IN A QUANTUM WORLD

The quantum era is a reality that is about to upend the cryptographic systems that support our digital world; it is no longer just a far-off prospect. With an emphasis on current research, readiness for developments in quantum computing, and long-term consequences for digital security, this chapter examines the future of cryptography in light of quantum innovations.

10.1 Continuous Innovation and Research

Researchers, governments, and commercial companies are all making significant investments in the search for strong security measures as the race to create quantum-resistant cryptography solutions heats up.

New Approaches to Quantum Resistance

Algorithms created to withstand the processing power of quantum machines are known as quantum-resistant, or post-quantum, encryption. Among the recent innovations are:

- **Lattice-Based Cryptography:** Algorithms such as Kyber and FrodoKEM use mathematical structures known as lattices, which give encryption and key exchange protocols a solid basis.

- **Code-Based Cryptography:** Methods such as the McEliece cryptosystem, which has been shown to be resilient against quantum attacks, employ error-correcting codes to guarantee security.

- **Hash-Based Cryptography:** SPHINCS+ and other hash-based cryptography systems are becoming more popular due to their effectiveness and little dependence on intricate mathematical difficulties.

- **Multivariate Polynomial Cryptography:** This field provides interesting uses for digital signatures and is centered on solving equations with several variables.

In order to ensure their suitability for broad deployment, several of these advances are being standardized through international programs such as the National Institute of

Standards and Technology's (NIST) post-quantum cryptography competition.

Research Investments in Cryptography

Innovations in post-quantum cryptography are being propelled by substantial investments:

- **Government Funding:** To guarantee that national infrastructure is safe against quantum threats, nations are spending billions on cybersecurity.
- **Academic Collaborations:** Universities around the world are leading the way in investigating cutting-edge cryptographic methods, connecting theoretical study with real-world implementations.

In order to prepare for commercial adoption, companies including Google, IBM, and Microsoft are integrating post-quantum technologies into their products.

AI's Contribution to Strengthening Cryptographic Defenses

In cryptography, artificial intelligence (AI) is becoming more and more important:

- Machine learning models examine possible flaws in cryptographic algorithms, spotting vulnerabilities before they can be exploited. This is known as AI-driven analysis.

- The development of quantum-resistant methods is being accelerated by the use of AI in the generation and testing of cryptographic systems.

- **Adaptive Security Protocols:** AI improves threat detection and response in real time, guaranteeing that cryptographic systems are resilient to changing attack scenarios.

The nexus of artificial intelligence and encryption will be a crucial area for innovation as the field of quantum computing develops.

10.2 Quantum Revolution Preparation

Although the exact moment of quantum supremacy is still unknown, it is obvious that preparation for its effects is urgent. Governments and organizations need to be proactive in order to guarantee cybersecurity readiness.

Timelines for Innovations in Quantum Computing

According to experts, a fully functional quantum computer that can crack popular encryption schemes might appear in the next ten to twenty years. Nonetheless, a few crucial elements could quicken this timeline:

- **Technological Advancements:** Constant enhancements to quantum hardware, including qubit stability and error correction.
- **More Funding:** Large sums of money from the public and private sectors.
- The collective endeavors of worldwide quantum computing projects constitute Collaborative Research.

Although precise dates are still up in the air, the possibility of an earlier discovery emphasizes the urgency of taking urgent action.

International Cybersecurity Readiness Initiatives

A coordinated worldwide reaction is necessary to counter

the quantum threat:

- **Standardization Initiatives:** The European Telecommunications Standards Institute (ETSI) and NIST are leading the charge to create standards for quantum-safe cryptography.

- **International Collaboration:** To guarantee coordinated defense strategy, governments and institutions are exchanging knowledge and best practices.

- **Legislative Measures:** To require the deployment of quantum-resistant protocols in important industries, regulatory frameworks are being changed.

Promoting Organizational Knowledge and Preparedness

Businesses need to adopt a strategic approach to quantum readiness:

- The process of determining which systems and assets are most susceptible to quantum attacks is known as risk assessment.

- **Educational Initiatives:** Educating staff members and interested parties about the consequences of post-quantum cryptography and quantum computing.

- **Early Adoption:** To guarantee a smooth transition, hybrid cryptographic systems that incorporate both conventional and quantum-resistant algorithms should be integrated.

The degree to which organizations can protect their operations and data in a future enabled by quantum technology will depend on their level of proactiveness.

10.3 Extended Consequences

Beyond short-term planning, quantum developments will have a significant impact on how digital systems and cryptography develop in the future.

Building Digital Systems for the Future

Taking proactive steps is necessary to guarantee the durability of cryptographic systems:

- **Scalable Solutions:** Post-quantum algorithms need to be flexible enough to change with the times.
- **Dynamic Cryptography:** Systems ought to provide

features for ongoing enhancements and modifications.

The ability of quantum-resistant protocols to smoothly integrate with current infrastructure is known as interoperability.

Businesses will be better prepared to handle the challenges of a quantum world if they embrace a future proofing approach.

Ethical Issues with Cryptographic Developments

The following ethical issues are brought up by the development of post-quantum cryptography and quantum computing:

- Privacy vs. Surveillance: As governments and businesses use sophisticated cryptographic techniques, it is critical to strike a balance between the rights of individuals to privacy and the objectives of national security.

- In order to prevent global cybersecurity inequality, it is important to make sure that small businesses and developing countries have access to quantum-resistant technologies.

- **Misuse of Quantum Technology:** Creating defenses against bad actors who might take use of quantum innovations for their own destructive ends.

For responsible development and implementation, ethical frameworks must advance with technology.

Making Sure Innovation and Security Are Balanced

Although security and innovation are frequently viewed as conflicting goals, they must coexist in the quantum era:

- Encouraging research and development of advanced cryptographic techniques is one way to drive innovation.
- **Preserving Security:** Making sure that advancements don't weaken the defenses of cryptography.
- **Encouraging Transparency**: Developing trust via transparent cooperation and standards that are subject to peer assessment.

Achieving this equilibrium will be essential for creating

robust systems that can adjust to the ever-changing demands of the quantum future.

For the field of cryptography, the quantum revolution offers previously unheard-of potential as well as obstacles. Strong, flexible, and morally sound cryptographic solutions are increasingly needed as quantum computing capabilities advance.

The future is becoming more secure thanks to the integration of artificial intelligence and the development of quantum-resistant algorithms.

- **Readiness for the Quantum Revolution**: To tackle new dangers, international cooperation and proactive organizational initiatives are crucial.
- **Long-Term Implications:** The development of cryptography in a world enabled by quantum technology will be determined by future-proofing systems, negotiating ethical issues, and striking a balance between innovation and security.

By adhering to these guidelines, we can make sure that, even in the face of revolutionary quantum developments, tomorrow's digital infrastructure is robust, safe, and fair.

ABOUT THE AUTHOR

 Author and thought leader in the IT field Taylor Royce is well known. He has a two-decade career and is an expert at tech trend analysis and forecasting, which enables a wide audience to understand complicated concepts.

Royce's considerable involvement in the IT industry stemmed from his passion with technology, which he developed during his computer science studies. He has extensive knowledge of the industry because of his experience in both software development and strategic consulting.

Known for his research and lucidity, he has written multiple best-selling books and contributed to esteemed tech periodicals. Translations of Royce's books throughout the world demonstrate his impact.

Royce is a well-known authority on emerging technologies and their effects on society, frequently requested as a speaker at international conferences and as a guest on tech podcasts. He promotes the development of ethical technology, emphasizing problems like data privacy and the digital divide.

In addition, with a focus on sustainable industry growth, Royce mentors upcoming tech experts and supports IT education projects. Taylor Royce is well known for his ability to combine analytical thinking with technical know-how. He sees a time when technology will ethically benefit humanity.